SAVING AN AMERICAN TREASURE
THE STORY OF VISTA HOUSE

KATHLEEN McMANUS OVERTON, PhD

Copyright © 2014

All rights reserved, including the right to reproduce this book or portions thereof in any form whatsoever.

Cover photo: Kenneth Overton

To

Marie Dorion
Heroine and Oregon's First Female Pioneer

and

Kenneth Michael Overton
Husband and Friend

and

Smokey
Furry Friend

Contents

Acknowledgements   3

Preface   9

IN THE BEGINNING

1
Context   13

2
Movers and Shakers   19

3
Vista House - The Structure   33

THE MIDDLE YEARS

4
Wear, Tear, and Neglect   61

5
Destructive Forces   69

6
Good Intentions   75

PRESENT DAY

7
Restoration   81

8
More Controversies   85

9
Rededication   93

APPENDICES

APPENDIX A
Vista House Awards   99

APPENDIX B
Vista House Association
Founders, 1916   103

APPENDIX C
Quotes from the Rotunda Columns and Walls   107

APPENDIX D
Pioneers Represented in
Vista House Rotunda   113

Sources   129

Acknowledgements

There are some who suggest not writing the acknowledgement section of a book because no one reads them. My own experience is different, so I did an extensive polling of eleven friends and found that some always do; some never read them; and for some, it depends.

Typical of many surveys, it told me what I already knew. Even if all eleven had responded that they never read this section of the book, I would have written it anyway, because this book would not be complete without a public recognition of the support that brought it to print.

The problem for me was where to begin. After a significant amount of time of writing nothing, I decided to begin chronologically. Thank you to Jim and Judi Hessel, wonderful friends, who introduced me to the Friends of Vista House organization. The Friends are the people who make Vista House come alive and share with the public the wonders of the building and the surrounding area. I consider it a privilege to be a part of their community.

One of many rewards in writing this book was the opportunity to work with people from many agencies who went out of their way to be helpful and assist me in the research shared here.

Those who stand out are Terry Baxter at Multnomah County Archives; Kimarie Lamb at the State Historic Preservation Office; and a number of the staff at Multnomah County Library. Equally important were people at the Oregon Historical Society, especially those in the research library. Their knowledge, accommodating attitudes, and support were beyond my expectations. Deserving of special attention are Scott Daniels, Reference Librarian and Scott Rook, Digital Assets Manager.

Then there are the gifted photographers who so generously allowed me to use their photographs: Sarah McDevitt for the ice photos; Matt Abinate for the night time image; Clem Bergevin for the wind in her hair shot; and for a number of different views of Vista House, Jim Hessel and Ken Overton, who also provided the cover photograph.

It is questionable to me whether or not this book would have come to fruition without the influence of a favorite author, Jane Kirkpatrick. Her wisdom and advice kept me going many times when I questioned continuing with the book.

Perhaps her most important guidance was to remember that this is my book, my story, not someone else's, and as a result it is just right. If someone thinks it should be done differently then they should write their own book. Jane has influenced me in many ways and I am grateful to have her in my life. One of Jane's suggestions was to attend her and Bob Welch's Beachside Writers Workshop in Yachats, Oregon, and I did in 2012.

After the previous two years of research, this experience gave me the courage to start writing. I think of myself as the cowardly lion in the Wizard of Oz, and the workshop, the Wizard who helped me find courage to formulate my research into a book.

Since that workshop both Jane and Bob have been available and supported my efforts. They each have published at least three excellent books in the year and a half since the workshop, I have managed to produce one – no wonder they are so inspiring.

Roger Hite, Ph.D. was one of the presenters at the Beachside Writers Workshop, sharing his expertise in self-publishing. Having produced over 30 books he understands the process and loves to share his knowledge with aspiring authors. Because of his spirit of generosity and skills in using Amazon's Create Space I was able to produce this book.

Thank you to all the family and friends who gave their support and encouragement throughout the research and writing, and there are too many to list them all individually. It would, however, be wrong to not name two of these people.

Edward and Claudia Brooks used their skills and talent to review and edit very early versions of the manuscript, resulting in a much-improved product. Claudia was also my advocate for the duration, aiding whenever needed. Few friends would make the commitment of time and energy to someone else's dream. For this and their friendship I feel blessed.

The need for a revision became clear shortly after the first printing was available. For the first revision of the book I am forever grateful to Drew and Annie Petersen and Will Summers, who shared their expertise, time, and support. Annie for her enthusiastic willingness to help, Drew for working miracles with the formatting, and Will for diligently applying his aptitude for correct grammar to vastly improve the text.

I also appreciate the Friends of Vista House Executive Director Marguerite Perry for taking the time to review the first edition and sharing her insights and edits.

As in the tradition of the theater to introduce the star of the show last, I thank my husband, Ken, who for over three years championed my writing this book. It was watching him as a docent at Vista House that inspired me to want to know more about the place he loved so much. He put as much time and commitment into the book as I did by not doing the things he would have liked to do, allowing me the time to do the research and write. He aided me by taking on many of the household duties and putting up with "make do" meals, or taking me out to dinner. These and so many other kindnesses and support were essential to the making of this book. And most important of all is his continuing love and friendship.

Preface

If you are reading this book the likelihood is that we have something in common: a love of books, an interest in history, questions about Vista House, and a wish to take something home to remind you of your journey. *Saving an American Treasure: The Story of Vista House* will satisfy all of these desires. After publishing the first book about Vista House, *Vista House: Crown of the Historic Columbia River Highway*, I realized a need for a revision. The book needed a new preface that focused attention to the bigger picture about the restoration of this American symbol of accomplishment.

All people over the age of 40 can remember some piece of the past that is no longer a tangible part of our heritage, something that they wish was still here to share with their friends, children or grandchildren. One of those losses for me is the destruction of Celilo Falls on the Columbia River, a place of beauty and the sacred and economic center for the Native American people. History comes alive when your five senses can respond to something, bringing a more complete experience of a place, event, or object. Our society is becoming satisfied with a virtual experience that is limiting the full awareness available when only the two senses, sight and hearing, are stimulated. This limited experience can be built upon by saving America's treasures for future generations to explore.

We owe a debt of gratitude to the people who crusade for saving those things of significance to our history which have contributed to our country's development and tell the story of what we have accomplished to become who we are. Vista House, like so many other symbols of where we have come from, deteriorated with time, use and neglect. However, Vista House, unlike so many other significant parts of our history, was saved from destruction and now is available so that we all can enjoy it and experience a part of our heritage.

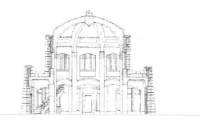

IN THE BEGINNING

1

Context

Samuel Lancaster wrote, "Our fondest dreams come true, if we work intelligently, earnestly, and with motives that are pure." Vista House is a testament to the truth of his wisdom.

Although best known for being the engineer of the Historic Columbia River Highway, Lancaster was also instrumental in the creation of Vista House and is credited with giving it its name. His dream was to have a structure built that would be the crowning achievement of his Columbia River Highway.

As testimony to his accomplishment of this goal one only has to consider the number of awards given to

Vista House, the most prestigious being placed on the National Register of Historic Places and being included in the Save America's Treasures program. (See Appendix A for additional information of these and other awards.)

Vista House is a legacy to be shared with future generations so they can see and understand a period of time when beauty triumphed over utility and the quality of work resulted in a creation of permanence instead of planned obsolescence.

The Vista House story could be told by conveying only the physical parameters of the building, the size, shape, architectural style, materials, etc., but these facts would never convey the dream aspects, or the significance and appreciation for one of our nation's icons.

Understanding the time period when Vista House was built is important in order to appreciate what a remarkable achievement it was.

In the early 1900s paved roads were almost unheard of, travel was done by horseback, buckboards, carriages, trains, bicycles, or if on water in a canoe or steamboat. The roads that were available were dirt, dusty when dry and, more likely in Oregon, mud when it was wet. The newly formed Oregon Good Road Association slogan in 1911 was,

"Let's Pull Oregon Out Of The Mud." Although few cars existed in the Northwest the interest in automobiles was increasing. In 1913 entrepreneur Sam Hill convinced the Multnomah County Commission of the need to build a road through the Columbia River Gorge in order to accommodate the transportation of goods from the eastern part of the Gorge to Portland, and to encourage tourism throughout the state.

Work began on the road in 1913, and by 1915 Lancaster realized he wanted to finish off the road with some sort of testament that would acknowledge the significance of the highway. He began the discussions about wanting to build this structure at a time when major world events were changing how people thought and lived.

The most significant development occurring at this time was the looming potential of US involvement in WWI. Although the US did not enter the war until April of 1917, the dread of war hung over the country like a black cloud before a hurricane.

Manufacturing demands for materials needed to support the war caused a growth of job opportunities resulting in an economic improvement from the recession of 1897. Once the U.S. entered the war, there was an even greater boom in industrial jobs. With over three and a half million men serving in the military, women were needed to fill both the peacetime and wartime jobs, providing them with new opportunities and forever changing the traditional role of wife, mother, and homemaker.

The 1910-1920 decade is known as a period of great change for America. The population in the US was approximately 93,000,000. In 1918 Oregon's population was over 783,000 with a life expectancy of around 55 years.

It was also the year law was passed requiring all children to attend elementary school, but only about ten percent completed high school. The price of a new home in 1915 was about $3,200 and the cost of a gallon of regular gas was 25 cents.

The first manufacturing assembly line began in 1914 and by 1915 the one millionth Model T Ford rolled off the line. Mass-production of the Model T which sold for $350.00, and the introduction of other car lines like Chevrolet, Dodge, and Nash, made it possible for the general population to own a car, thus creating a need for more and better roads.

By 1916 there were about 34,000 cars registered in all of Oregon and about 2.5 million in the nation. Today's estimate is over 250 million registered vehicles in the US.

The early 20th century was also the period of the suffragettes, women who were considered militant because of their actions to gain women's right to vote. One of these actions was to change their dress to a more comfortable fashion and to stand out and be noticed. They accomplished this by wearing lighter more colorful fabrics and higher hemlines that went so far as to show the ankles, and perhaps the most provocative, wearing pants.

Popular toys were Lincoln Logs, Erector Sets, and Tinker Toys. People were reading books by Emily Dickinson, Willa Cather, Zane Gray, and Carl Sandberg as well as appreciating art by Georgia O'Keeffe, Max Weber, and Norman Rockwell. The fox trot and tango were dance crazes, with ragtime, blues, and jazz popular categories of music. The presidents for this era were William Howard Taft, 1909-1913, and Woodrow Wilson, 1913-1921.

2

Movers and Shakers

> We are the music-makers,
> And we are the dreamers of dreams,
> Wandering by lone sea-breakers,
> And sitting by desolate streams;
> World-losers and world-forsakers,
> On whom the pale moon gleams:
> Yet we are the movers and shakers
> Of the world forever, it seems
>
> ALFRED O'SHAUGHNESSY, ODE, 1873

Without the "movers and shakers" of the world many dreams would not come true, and a great number of the things we treasure might never have come to fruition.

The grandeur of the Columbia River Gorge is rightfully referred to as awe-inspiring, and the word inspiring is also appropriate for the men who were responsible for the Columbia River Highway and Vista House. Without the Columbia River Highway there would have been no reason for Vista House.

A number of the people who made the highway possible were also the ones who determined a need for the building and were responsible for it getting built. The most notable of those people were Sam Hill, Sam Lancaster, John Yeon, and Edgar Lazarus, each contributing unique visionary and creative genius, and in some cases monetary assistance.

SAM HILL - VISIONARY

Although Sam Hill was not directly involved in the building of Vista House, it would not have been built if he had not convinced the appropriate people of the need for the Columbia River Highway. He is truly one of those bigger than life individuals who made things happen wherever he went.

Sam was well described in an interview with John B. Yeon's son who stated, "I admired him enormously because he was the only one around with a large-scale romantic imagination."

Hill was born May 13, 1857, in Deep River, North Carolina. His family was active in the anti-slavery movement and played a part in the Underground Railroad, which led to their need to move from the area, choosing to go to Minneapolis, Minnesota.

After finishing his undergraduate work he received a Bachelor's Degree from Haverford University, a Quaker College located just outside of Philadelphia, and then attended Harvard University earning a law degree.

Following graduation, he returned to Minneapolis and began his career in 1886 as a litigator for James J. Hill, the head of the Great Northern Railway and one of the most powerful men in transportation. (Although the last names were the same, the Hills were not related.) Sam married Mary Hill, James' eldest daughter.

Sam Hill's success over the next decade made him a wealthy and influential businessman, and he was known for his civic mindedness and honesty. Always the adventurer, Sam wanted to become independent and branch out into other interests, choosing Seattle, Washington, as the place to pursue new opportunities. He moved his family to Seattle but in short order his wife found it unbearable.

Over a period of years Mary Hill traveled back and forth from Minnesota to Seattle but eventually made a permanent move back to live with her father and mother in Minneapolis. Although never divorced, Sam and his wife did not live together for the remainder of their lives. His wife and daughter both suffered from mental health problems and some believe Sam exhibited bipolar behavior.

Hill ventured into numerous undertakings some of which were very successful and others that were failures. His greatest passion was the Good Roads Movement, founded in 1880 to encourage national support for better roads for bicyclists.

When the interest in bicycles waned in favor of the new gas propelled automobile the focus of the movement shifted to creating paved cross-country roads to support automobile traffic.

Mr. Hill committed his unlimited energy, creative mind, and financial support to assuring better roads for both Oregon and Washington. He is quoted in the book, *Sam Hill: Prince of Castle Nowhere*, as saying, "Good roads are more than my hobby, they are my religion."

SAMUEL C. LANCASTER - ENGINEER

Sam Hill was responsible for Sam Lancaster becoming the design engineer of the Columbia River Highway. Without Hill and Lancaster there would be no Columbia River Highway and thus no Vista House. The word remarkable is not encompassing enough to describe Lancaster. He was a man of contrasts who was gifted with the mind of an engineer, a heart of a poet, and the spirit of a warrior.

Samuel Lancaster was born in 1864 in Magnolia, Mississippi. He only finished one year of college, but learned engineering skills working with the chief engineer of the Illinois Central Railroad. While in his early 20s and working in the Yazoo-Mississippi Delta, he contracted malaria and later was afflicted with infantile paralysis (polio) that left him paralyzed from the neck down.

In spite of his doctor believing he would never regain his mobility, Lancaster was committed to finding ways to be less of an invalid. He learned to draw with his mouth, allowing him to apply his engineering skills to sketch a castered frame to hold himself upright and let him use his toes to painfully move around the house. Eventually he decided to try to stand alone without the frame, but collapsed on the floor engulfed in agonizing pain.

As a result of the fall he found some flexibility had returned to the frozen tendons in his crippled toes. Sam realized the fall was an answer to his prayers for regaining his mobility. By shear force he proceeded with the torturous process of unlocking all the frozen tendons in his body.

One can only imagine the excruciating pain he experienced in order to gain back his mobility. His efforts were so rewarding that during the design of the highway he was actively involved in climbing and repelling the basalt cliffs of the Columbia River Gorge.

Throughout the surveying process there are numerous accounts regarding Lancaster's commitment to maintaining the beauty of the Gorge, while designing a road that allowed travelers the opportunity to see and appreciate the beauty of this land.

He described his intention for the road when he wrote,

> On starting the surveys, our first business was to find the beauty spots, or those points where the most beautiful things along the line might be seen to the best advantage, and if possible to locate the road in such a way as to reach them.

At the same time he wanted to accomplish this with the least amount of damage to the environment. Many consider Lancaster one of the first engineering environmentalists.

Even before the completion of the Highway, Lancaster knew he wanted to see a structure that would represent a crown for his "King of America's highways." He envisioned an observation point that would allow visitors a place for protection from the elements where they could view the unique beauty of the Gorge, "in silent communication with the infinite."

In 1915 he began his campaign for the building and suggested that it be called Vista House and be built on Thor's Heights, or what is now called Crown Point. Lancaster also contributed ideas for the design of the building, especially for the interior.

Although a number of his ideas were not carried out, he certainly had a substantial impact on the building of Vista House.

JOHN B. YEON – CONSTRUCTION MANAGER

Another of the important and resourceful people involved in the design of the Columbia River Highway and in the construction of Vista House is John Baptiste Yeon. He was a French-Canadian, born in

Plantagenet, Ontario, April 24, 1865. He came to Portland, Oregon, in 1885 from lumber camps in Ohio.

According to his son, Yeon eventually saved enough money to start buying timber that yielded him sufficient income to invest in Portland real estate. The younger Yeon referred to his father's rise to prominence as being done in a Horatio Alger fashion, going from rags to riches by hard work, honesty, and giving back to his community.

After Lancaster was selected as engineer for the Columbia River Highway, John Yeon was appointed as the Multnomah County Roadmaster. His responsibility was overseeing the construction of the Columbia River Highway, and supervising a work crew of over 2,000 men. When asked to take on this position Yeon's reported response was, "I'll build the roads. I will act as county Roadmaster for one year without salary. But you couldn't hire me for this job for $1500 a month."

Lancaster appreciated and respected Yeon's experience managing logging camps and knew that John understood the standard of excellence that he expected. Mr. Lancaster referred to him as

> a wealthy and public-spirited citizen
> of Portland (who) volunteered to
> give, without remuneration, his en-

tire time to this splendid work; and his offer was quickly accepted.

Mr. Yeon's long experience in handling men in lumber camps fitted him admirably for this great task. His sagacity and love of the beautiful enabled him to grasp the meaning of the Engineer's plans, and thus to decide important matters correctly and with great dispatch.

Because of his exceptional work on the highway and his appreciation for maintaining the beauty of the Gorge, he was reappointed Roadmaster and took on the responsibility for overseeing the building of Vista House.

EDGAR LAZARUS - ARCHITECT

On June 6, 1868, Edgar Jr. was born in Charleston, S.C. His father, Edgar Sr., served in the Confederate Army. His mother, Minnie, was the daughter of Moses Mordecai, a wealthy merchant. The Lazarus family moved to Baltimore in 1867, where they became involved in the Baltimore society. Edgar Jr. attended Maryland Institute of Art and Design and graduated from the Architecture Department in 1888. Following graduation he was hired by the US Army and designed military buildings until 1891, when he moved to Portland, Oregon.

Shortly after arriving in Portland he and another architect, William Ellicott, formed the Ellicott and Lazarus architectural firm. They were responsible for designing buildings for the Oregon Institute for the Blind, Multnomah Amateur Athletic Club, and the Maryland University Hospital of Baltimore. Lazarus is also credited with the design of several other buildings including a number of beautiful homes in the Portland area. All in all, he was responsible for the design of over 150 buildings during his 40-year career.

Outside of his role as architect, Edgar Lazarus was well established in the social circles of Portland. He was a member of a number of prominent clubs, including being a founding member of the Vista House Association, a Charter member of the Oregon Road Club, founding member of the Oregon Chapter of the American Institute of Architects, and, the Portland Architectural Club. Mr. Lazarus was a strong supporter of the Portland Art Museum, even loaning personal items for exhibitions, as well as the Jewish community. In his leisure time he owned and raced horses, and was actively involved in the racing and sports community.

One of the benefits of membership in many different organizations and involvement with influential people of Portland society was the opportunity to meet people in need of an architect. His networking brought him in contact with Sam Lancaster, Sam Hill, and John Yeon. When it came time to select an architect for Vista House, knowing the right people, and having a reputation for exceptional work, made Lazarus an easy choice.

In addition to being a prominent Portland architect Lazarus was also an interesting and colorful individual. Not shy about sharing his opinions, he frequently expressed them in public places like *The Oregonian*, Portland's major newspaper, on subjects such as not limiting the amount of noise youngsters can make on the 4th of July, and his concern for the growing state debt.

Perhaps the most interesting articles were his responses to reports regarding his battles for payment for his services with both the State and Multnomah County. The most contentious episode was with the State concerning payment for his work on the State Hospital. Although the work began in 1909, the newspaper documentation of problems really began in October 1917 when the Board of Control sent a letter to *The Oregonian* accusing Lazarus of graft. From that point on the proverbial fur was flying.

Lazarus' response to the letter outlined his many grievances with the State's failure to meet their contractual agreements regarding payment and scope of work for a number of buildings he and his firm designed. Although there are always two sides to a story, Edgar Lazarus had good documentation of the contractual agreement where it is stated he would receive a fee of 5% of the total cost of the buildings.

It wasn't until after his initial payment that he found the actual total cost was significantly higher than the figure his payment had been calculated on. Lazarus requested additional payment for the difference, approximately $23,000 in today's dollars.

During this time, Lazarus was also under contract with Multnomah County to design and oversee the building of Vista House. This contract was made with John Yeon as a representative of the Board Commissioners for a 10% fee based on the total cost of the building. This agreement would later become a matter of discontent among some Board members.

As the costs for Vista House started to exceed the original estimates first accepted by the Board, Lazarus' projected compensation also increased. When the total cost of building Vista House far exceeded the original estimate he became involved in another dispute over being paid on the basis of the total cost of the project, this time with Multnomah County. After three years of dispute, Lazarus filed suit against the county, but was essentially unsuccessful.

If this wasn't enough, Lazarus also found himself immersed in conflict with his professional organization after accusing some of the other members of unethical behavior. Before it was over, he resigned and essentially dropped out of the architectural scene.

His life took on a new focus after retirement. While visiting his brothers in New Jersey, he met Fanny Hendricks, a wealthy, prominent women in New Jersey society. Not long after, they were married on November 17, 1921. Both being people of means, they spent their lives together traveling around the world and frequently were the focus of Portland society. Edgar Lazarus died on October 2, 1939 in Portland, Oregon at the age of seventy-one.

VISTA HOUSE ASSOCIATION

These movers and shakers were the ones who stood out the most from the many people who contributed to the inception of Vista House. Although much enthusiasm was generated for going ahead with the building there was a need for organizing the efforts that resulted in a number of prominent Portland businessmen forming the Vista House Association.

Their goal was to generate the necessary funding for the design, construction, and materials cost of the building. A number of fund raising campaigns were planned but in the end they were unsuccessful and most all of the cost ended up being financed by Multnomah County, albeit not without controversy. (See Appendix for a list of the founding members.)

3

Vista House - The Structure

To fulfill Lancaster's dream of a structure that would represent a crown for his "King of American Highways" and would also function as an "isle of safety to all visitors who wish to look on that matchless scene," was certainly a big enough challenge for Mr. Lazarus, but there is more to the story. While Lancaster was gathering up support for a building that would be the crowning glory for his highway, another need had been identified. The story goes that Julius Meier (partner of the Meier and Frank department stores, and later to become Oregon's governor) had taken a group of women for a ride to show them the new Columbia River Highway, during which time it became clear that long trips

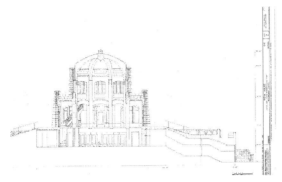

Vista House Plan—Permission granted by Oregon Historical Society Research Library. Vista House Architectural Plan Section C-C Looking West. Historical Engineering Record, Heritage Conservation and Recreation Service, Patricia Fletcher and Ann Beth Koval, 1981

without a "rest stop" was not going to work. Following the trip he immediately met with the Multnomah County board to seek funding for this necessity. As discussions followed, it was suggested that since there was no significant memorial to Oregon's pioneers, and that Crown Point overlooking the Columbia River where many of them traveled, would be an ideal site for such a memorial structure. In the end Lazarus was charged with designing a building that would be a crown for the highway and isle of safety for travelers, an appropriate rest stop for ladies, and a fitting memorial to Oregon pioneers!

The ground breaking for the building was June 7, 1916, the same day as the dedication of the Columbia River Highway. Horses, wagons, and carts hauled the building materials and Fresno scrapers, drawn by two horses, were used to excavate the site. Concrete was mixed and hauled by hand using the limited equipment of the period.

Vista House - The Structure

Vista House during construction—Photo, permission granted by Oregon Historical Society Research Library. Negative number 00439 (Women and children pose on Stones Cut for Vista House)

Even so, it took less than two years to complete the building. Just think about the time it would take today to build a structure of such complexity and beauty using all the latest state of the art equipment. It would probably take two years just to get permits signed.

VISTA HOUSE – THE EXTERIOR

When looking at Vista House one is given the impression of a cathedral or castle, something of great significance like a crown worn by royalty. Words do not adequately describe the unique impression given by a structure of such grandeur. Each

Close up of Vista House—Photo courtesy of Jim Hessel

individual element deserves attention and when integrated together is nothing less than remarkable.

Vista House's distinctive architecture is often referred to as Art Nouveau or the Jungendstil style, but the architect, Edgar Lazarus, described it as Tudor Gothic. Lazarus' training had been in the classical Beaux Arts School, and he also drew from elements of Gothic, Art Nouveau, and Arts and Crafts models.

In 2011 Edward Teague, of the University of Oregon School of Architecture, evaluated the design. He reported that the octagonal features reflect the Gothic style, and the level of workmanship is more aligned with the Arts and Crafts movement, but there is little reflecting Art Nouveau characteristics.

Perhaps Vista House is best described as being more of a distinct design than a singular style.

The domed, octagonal-shaped building rests on a basalt bluff created by lava flows and shaped by the Ice Age Floods and extreme weather. Local residents referred to the land it is built on as Thor's Heights after the Germanic mythological god Thor, the god of thunder and storms. At the time of the building of the Columbia River Highway the area became known as Crown Point acknowledging Lancaster's need to crown his "king of roads." Mr. and

Basalt Bluffs—Photo courtesy of Kenneth Overton

Mrs. Lorenz Lund generously donated the property in 1914 to the City of Portland. The structure sits 733 feet above the river, is 44' in diameter, 55' high, and has a substructure, or lower level, which is 64' in diameter. The exterior is reinforced concrete that is faced with a light gray ashlar Tenino Sandstone façade that was mined near Wilkeson, Washington. Surrounding the building are circular concrete steps now with a curved ramp for Americans with Disabilities Act (ADA) accessibility that was added in 2005. The walkway at the top of the stairs has periodic sections of glass bricks that allow natural light into the basement.

The rock wall supporting the sidewalk around the building shows two types of construction. One is a dry-ma-

Rock wall face supporting Vista House sidewalk—author photo

View east from Vista House balcony—author photo

sonry technique and the other using cement to reinforce the stone. A story is told that men from Italy were brought here specifically to do the specialized work, but more likely they were Italian dry-masons living in Portland, Oregon. You can see a line of demarcation between the two techniques in the photo, dry masonry on the right, and cemented wall on the left.

The top story of the building is a balcony walkway that allows visitors an unobstructed view of the Columbia River flowing through the geologic wonder of the Gorge. On a clear day one can see 40 miles looking east, west and north. Looking south the view is limited by Larch Mountain. Some have correlated walking around the balcony to

View west from Vista House balcony—author photo

Vista House at night—photo courtesy of Matt Abinate

walking around the crown of the Statute of Liberty - but with a more breathtaking landscape. The roof is covered in stunning matte-glazed green terra cotta tiles made by the Ludowici Tile Company in Lexington, Ohio. The color of the tiles was intended to complement the vast multi-colored green landscape.

The road circling below Vista House has a viaduct supporting a sidewalk along the highway. Placed along a protective wall are concrete columns made to hold twenty-nine light fixtures that give the impression of a crown when glowing at night; fulfilling Lancaster's goal for a building that would express,

Vista House South Entrance—author photo

> The silent dignity of the pavilion, with its outline against the sky,

will recall the ancient mystic Thor's crown, which the point was originally named.

VISTA HOUSE - THE INTERIOR

The Vista House structure is a unique shape that captures the curiosity and invites one to come inside to see what is housed in such a marvelous piece of architecture. Those curious folk who accept the invitation will find that the exterior is the enticement to the awe-inspiring artistry of the interior. Stepping inside the rotunda is as if entering an intimate cathedral, creating a sense of something hallowed, a place of significance.

Vista House rotunda—photo courtesy of Kenneth Overton

Interpretative pannel on column in Vista House rotunda—author photo. (Text from the panels and columns is in Appendix C)

As the initial impression moves to the specifics of the room one sees the Alaskan Tokeen marble floor tiles aligned true north, with a central circular design aligned magnetic north (17 degrees from true north) for added creative detail.

The Vermont Marble Company supplied the marble that was mined on the Prince of Wales Island located on Davidson Inlet, in Alaska.

The same marble trims the base of eight Kasota limestone columns that support the roof beams of the elegant dome. The Kasota stone was mined in Minnesota. Each of the columns is inscribed with attractive interpretive information about the Columbia River Gorge, the Historic Highway, Oregon pioneers, Native Americans of the area, and Vista House.

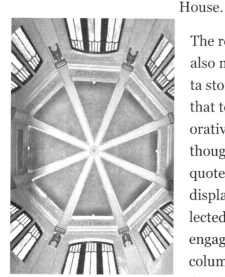

Rodunda dome—photo courtesy of Kenneth Overton

The rotunda walls are also made of Kasota stone and plaster that today have decorative panels with thought-provoking quotes and vials for the display of privately collected wildflowers. The engaging quotes on the columns and walls add depth to the perspective of Vista House and the Gorge. (See Appendix C for the quotations from the wall panels.)

As one bends their head back and their eyes bring into focus the artisanship of the interior dome, it becomes apparent that the creators of the building wanted to bestow a sense of elegance fit for the viewing of the grandeur of the Columbia River Gorge. The dome ceiling and supporting ribs were originally planned to be marble and bronze, but because of the excessive costs they are reinforced concrete with a plaster finish, painted to simulate marble and bronze.

Indian head sculpture—photo courtesy of Jim Hessel

At the top of the eight columns supporting the dome are bronze-like sculptures representing the indigenous people of the area. There are four different likenesses each with a mirror image directly across from it that are cast in plaster and painted instead of being bronze as originally planned. It is not known if the sculptures are of specific individuals. Some have speculated that because Sam

Hill had been named as honorary chief of the Nez Perce tribe and Lancaster commits a number of pages of his book, *The Columbia: America's Great Highway*, to Chief Joseph and Northwest Indians, the sculpture may have been from this tribe. At this time it is believed that the sculptures are representations rather than specific individuals.

Besides being one of the outstanding features of the rotunda, the figures are also significant in their placement in the room. Located at the top of the columns bearing the weight of the dome is architecturally significant of strength, and recognizes the importance of Oregon's first residents, Native Americans. It is interesting that one of the most frequently asked questions is about the identity of the sculptures.

Pioneer shield (Lee) with Indian heads and stain glass windows—author photo

In keeping with the intent of designating Vista House as a monument to early Oregon Pioneers, centered between each of the columns are plaster panels with the carved names of eight Oregon pioneers: Dr. John McLoughlin, Jesse Applegate, James Nesmith, Joseph Lane, Asahel Bush, Matthew Deady, Rev. Jason Lee and Marcus Whitman. (For more information on these pioneers, see Appendix D)

Frederick V. Holman, who then was president of the Oregon Historical Society, and George H. Hines, who was curator of that organization and secretary of the Oregon Pioneer Association are credited with the selection of the names to represent the hardy people who first populated the Oregon Territory.

Accompanying the names of the pioneers in the rotunda are depictions of plants and tools used by the pioneers. The plants represented are all found in Oregon: chestnut, oak acorns, pine cones, grape, apple, wheat, Oregon grape, and ginkgo. The tools represent implements that the pioneers used to settle in the area: a hoe, wheelbarrow, pickaxe, shovel, scythe, and watering can.

Equally as spectacular as the rest of the building are the marvelous opalescent stained glass window. On the main floor, each of the eight sets of windows are either all art glass, or in the main viewing areas clear glass allowing visitors an unobstructed view of Mother Nature's sculpturing of the Columbia Gorge

Vista House - The Structure

Water Fountain—Photo courtesy of Kenneth Overton

- beautiful at any time and extraordinary on a sunny day.

If one is fortunate enough to be there in the late afternoon on a sunny day, as the sun descends towards the Pacific, the light hits the windows causing the glass to come alive. The colors glow and change becoming so vibrant it feels like you are witnessing the very creation of beauty.

Unobtrusively attached to the two south columns are hand carved Kasota stone drinking water fountains that are so attractive you want to take a drink even if you are not thirsty. Besides providing travelers easy access to quench their thirst, the quality of the fixtures enhances the elegance of the building.

Behind the fountains are staircases with cast iron balustrades and brass handrails. One set ascends to the upper level of the building where

Ascending Staircase—author photo

there is an open walkway allowing viewers to circle the dome, providing a view of the Columbia River and the Gorge. Even though the balcony is a favorite part of the Vista House, it can be closed for safety reasons when it is wet and or windy.

After returning to the main floor, it is time to take the staircase that goes to the lower level of the building where you find, arguably, the most important feature of the building, the restrooms.

Descending Staircase—author photo

Women's restroom—author photo

When you enter the restroom, you are standing on a terrazzo floor (a composite material made of marble and a cementitious material) with wainscoting walls made of the same Alaska marble used throughout the building. Toilet stalls are marble with straight-grained Mahogany doors hung with brass hinges. But most impressive in 1918 were the flush toilets and sinks with running water! No big deal today, but in 1918, when it was common for homes to have outhouses instead of indoor plumbing, it was beyond exceptional to find a building with, what was then, this modern convenience.

Men's restroom—photo courtesy of Kenneth Overton

Even the water closets were selected with great care. They were the top of the line Crane Company "Purus" siphon jet bowl toilets with air controlled flushing valve, the most innovative system of the time. (The Crane Co. was established in 1855 and is still considered one of the leaders of the industry.)

Equally important were the fan ventilation and the heating system needed for the months of colder weather. An interesting fact is that Vista House is the first roadside rest stop in the nation. A Crane Company article referred to it as, "the most picturesque and best appointed public highway comfort station in the country, if not, indeed, in the world."

Although an important feature of the lower level, the restrooms are just part of the offerings to

Clockwise from top: **Outside view of tunnel entrance**—photo, permission granted by Oregon Historical Society Research Library. Negative number 004324 (One man stands by lower level entrance); **Inside tunnel**—photo courtesy of Kenneth Overton; **Curved hallways panels**—author photo be found in the unique circular hallways of Vista House. At the north end of the building there is a tunnel leading to an outside door that was originally intended to drop off the ladies who wanted to use the facilities and freshen up. The story is that gentlemen would drive their cars parallel to the tunnel entrance, help the ladies out, leaving them only a few steps away from easy access with little exposure to the weather. The lounges were available to freshen up, dust off, and rearrange one's attire. Today the lounges are serving different purposes.

Proceeding with the exploration of the lower level you continue to see the same elegant materials used in the other areas of the building. The commitment to the highest quality products is as apparent in this level as it is in the rotunda. The hallway is laid out in a circular pattern that takes visitors to the tunnel, interpretative displays, concession area, and the men and women's lounges that were originally attached to the restrooms.

Along the hallway there are attractive interpretative panels that tell the history of the area and what was happening around the time Vista House was built. Continuing on through the hallway there is a concession area and gift shop. After Vista House was opened the sales area was run by Cross and Dimmitt, who were well known for their photogra-

Clockwise from top left: **Section of interpretative panel re: car camping**—author photo; **Coffee Shop**—photo, courtesy of Kenneth Overton; **Gift Shop book selection**—author photo; **Gift Shop misc. items**—author photo

phy, and sold many of their photographs as penny postcards. (Today those penny postcards are collectors' items, one recently being priced at $50.) Besides the postcards the concessions provided refreshments and popular souvenirs. Today the concessions are run by the Friends of Vista House who provide refreshments, like espresso coffees, tea, and ice cream in the Coffee Shop and in the Gift Shop items by artists of the Northwest, books, jewelry, and, some souvenirs. All of the proceeds from the Gift and Coffee shops go to support the Friends' commitment to caring for Vista House.

As visitor traffic flows in the circular pattern around the central restrooms, one is struck by the uniqueness of the design. The marble on the floors and walls glisten as the light comes through the glass brick skylights. One section of the hallway, the mechanical and business area, is closed to the public.

CONTROVERSIES

Like life, the building of Vista House did not come about without its controversies. The disagreements were not just misunderstandings, but disputes that went to court and, in one case, even came to a physical altercation.

Arguments over costs started heating up during the April 1916 meetings of the Multnomah County Commission. When the Board was asked to approve $12,000 from emergency road funds to be used along with $6,000 raised by the Vista House Association for building the substructure, a few of the commissioners voiced strong concerns.

Although there were mixed opinions about using County money, and about whether or not the structure should even be built, the majority of commissioners approved the request and building began in the latter part of 1916. However, it wasn't long before John Yeon, Roadmaster and Project Manager, was back asking for additional funding.

This new request, and numerous others, was for money to build two levels above the substructure and for design changes. When the appeals were periodically brought to the commission the majority of commissioners approved each one. On July 22, 1917 an article in *The Oregonian* indicated that at least one commissioner did not support the approval and that the costs were out of control because of a lack of,

> ...any definite conception beyond making it a fit accessory to the highway. The adoption of a certain feature gave birth to another until the

whole scheme expanded to it present proportions.

In the end, instead of costing the initial estimate of $18,000, the total cost was just short of $100,000.

Even though the majority of commissioners approved each request, Board Chairman, Rufus Holman, was adamant that it was a misuse of the County's budget. In addition, in April 1916, the Taxpayers' League and a number of citizens protested the expenditures. Some people not only felt it was an inappropriate use of their tax dollars, but believed that the Board did not have the authority to approve such allocation.

At the County Commission meeting in March 1917, Commissioner Holman submitted a lengthy objection to the Road Department's recommended budget, stating in part:

> I feel that we must preserve some funds for an unforeseen emergency or a disaster, should we be confronted with such a calamity. Who knows but that before the year is out this nation may be engaged in war? What local administrative body, if not Multnomah County, will be prepared to care for the families of our local soldiers and be able to respond to such similar demands? Should we not protect some of our cash resources for such contingencies?

In spite of the objection, the Commission ordered that the entire road department budget, including the allocation for Vista House, be accepted.

The discord persisted throughout construction and even after. Holman continued to contend that spending this enormous amount of taxpayer money on a "toilet facility" was unconscionable. The battles played out in local newspapers, with reports of name-calling and fighting that resulted in Chairman Holman requesting a police presence at future sessions of the Board of Commissioners.

Many accusations were made and at least two lawsuits filed. Although both suits were dismissed, the discord resulted in continued hard feelings and probably contributed to the resignation of John Yeon as Roadmaster.

In the end, building Vista House cost almost $100,000. The June, 1918 issue of the *Oregon Historical Quarterly* shows the breakdown of the total cost for Vista House: $70,788: building; rockwork: $9,297; grading and paving: $7,385; architect: $6,264; miscellaneous: $2,976, for a total $96,710 at a time when people were receiving a good wage of $2,200 a year.

1918 VISTA HOUSE DEDICATION

"All Portland Pays Homage to Pioneers - Vista House Dedicated at Crown Point" reads a front-page article in *The Oregonian* newspaper on May 6, 1918. W.H. Perkins wrote a beautifully descriptive article that sets the mood for all of the day's pageantry:

> Silent it (Vista House) stands -a gray cameo cut from the imperishable cliffs. At times, the trailing mists that follow up the great river swirl around its thick walls, blotting them from view. At morn, the Herald of Day throws aside the robes of night and paints its eastern windows with many a penciled shaft; at night he crowns it with a golden glory.

Today's standard of news reporting makes this passage seem a bit embellished and flowery but it certainly was fitting for the grandeur of the dedication. The day began at noon in downtown Portland with a gathering of over 200 automobiles that paraded up to Crown Point for the celebration.

Police indicated that over 1500 cars actually visited the site throughout the day. The attendees included some of the most prominent people of Portland including the Governor, many other dignitaries, and thousands of other celebrants.

1918 Vista House Dedication—photo, permission granted from Oregon Historical Society Research Library. Negative number 002761

Also in attendance were Civil War veterans, a squad of soldiers of the 443rd Squadron, Signal Corps. Three women who survived as children in the Whitman massacre of 1847 also attended. Eloquent speeches were given about the building, the people responsible for it, and the Oregon pioneers.

The Royal Rosarians, Portland's Ambassadors of Goodwill, played a major role in the ceremony, looking elegant in their white suits and straw hats. Their band and quartet provided the prescribed musical pageantry that the occasion deserved.

When it came time for the traditional champagne toast, elderberry juice was substituted in order to adhere to Oregon's 1915 alcohol prohibition law.

The day ended with the unfurling of the same flag that was used earlier for the dedication of the Columbia River Highway. For the 1916 Highway dedication, the flag was unfurled by the press of an electronic button by President Wilson from the

White House. Many years later the flag was given to the Friends of Vista House for display.

> And Vista House, a part of the very cliff itself, shall lift its portals of stone above the mists for a thousand years. And the great waters shall flow by, unvexed by war or warriors, and the forest shall whisper the never-fading deeds of those who came and planted and reaped among the hills and the valleys of the Westland.
>
> W.H. PERKINS (REPORTER FOR *THE OREGONIAN*)

THE MIDDLE YEARS

4

Wear, Tear, and Neglect

Since its dedication in 1918, Vista House has drawn many millions of people from all over the world. Whether you call them visitor, guest, tourist, or traveler, people who come to Vista House have an opportunity to not only take in the view but to learn about the history of the building; history and geology of the area; the waterfalls and hiking trails in the Gorge; directions to other areas such as places to eat and gas stations; all provided by interpretative volunteers. These Friends of Vista House volunteers/docents provide a choice between a cursory or comprehensive history, depending on the guest's level of interest. The focus of the interpretative volunteers is to help the visitor enjoy and learn about what they came to see, and provide opportunities for creating lifetime memories.

Entries in the guest book at the interpreter's desk reflect the impressions left on the people who have come from every continent and from every state in the USA. Comments like "Feeling close to God"; "God's amazing beauty"; "My soul is nurtured"; and in a texting format, "OMG" (Oh my God) reflect the mystical impact on some, while entries such as: "Never seen anything like it"; "Awesome is an understatement"; "History come alive", and "Windy, dramatic, beyond description" indicate the more tangible responses.

Perhaps the most colorful comment came from a reporter in 1926 traveling with Queen Mary of Bulgaria. Waiting for the Queen while she visited the Vista House powder room, it is reported that he, "placed his hand up to his ear, then he snapped his fingers and said, "That's it men, the Royal Flush."

In addition to providing the interpretative resources to answer questions there are concessions to supply travelers with food and drink and a store full of unique art items.

In his original plans Edgar Lazarus spoke of using space for selling items that would support the traveler's journey. As years went on, questions were raised when commercialized sales became more of a focus than providing what was considered by some as the intent for the building: "a shelter and sanctuary for the traveler to commune with the beauty of the Gorge."

In 1958 the owners of a restaurant across from Vista House, Montford and Janice Moore, brought suit against the State Highway Commission and Vista House concessionaire, Jack A. Flaucher, seeking closure of the business. They alleged that concessions violated terms agreed upon when the land was donated. However, Lawrence Lund, who originally donated the land to Multnomah County, testified in defense of the State, indicating that concessions had been in place since the opening of Vista House and were a part of the architect's original design.

The State Superintendent of Parks testified that loss of the concessions and the $8,000 to $10,000 a year income they brought in would possibly force the closure of Vista House, because the state would not be able to pay for all of the custodial and repair costs.

In the end it was ruled that the concessions would remain, but it was also noted that the State had neglected the building and that the commercial activities had become too predominant.

FRIENDS OF VISTA HOUSE

Thankfully, the concessions were allowed to continue and provide revenue to help keep Vista House open. But it was not enough to maintain an adequate level of care the building needed.

After years of use, misuse, and neglect, the building fell into such disrepair that closing it permanently or even needing to tear it down was considered. The once elegant crown of Thor's Heights was now a worn-out tiara.

In 1980, for safety concerns, Oregon State Parks closed the concessions and the lower level, except the restrooms. Following the closure, members of the community of Corbett, Oregon, came together and established the Vista House Project. The group met with Parks representatives to determine the possibility of opening Vista House as a gallery for local artists to show and sell their work. Their first attempts were met with skepticism, but after months of discussions there was an agreement to open part of the building as an information and art resource. Any surplus money, after the artists were paid, was to be used for restoring and supporting building programs.

Then in 1982, in cooperation with State Parks, volunteers spent months cleaning and repairing the shambles that had resulted from the neglect over the years. In the rotunda, floors were scrubbed clean; brass work was cleaned and polished; windows washed; and, overall, much needed maintenance was tended to, bringing the once dignified rotunda back to some level of its former beauty.

The lower level remained in a state of disrepair. Having been used primarily as storage space the site might make one think of a packrat's den or the beginning of a hoarder's refuge. Beside sheer neglect, water seepage had eaten away at the plasterwork, and the emissions from the oil furnace covered everything.

When entering the area, one was assaulted with the smells of deteriorating plaster, mold, and oil. Credit goes to the local volunteers who took on the Herculean task to restore the conditions so the basement once again would be available to visitors.

The payback for all the admirable efforts was the summer opening of an information desk and a small gallery with local handcrafted gifts. Although the season was short, it was successful, and because of this success the shop area increased and the volunteer interpretive program expanded to full time.

In 1987 the Oregon State Legislature's approved the formation of "Friends" organizations. Friends groups are utilized throughout the United States to support the activities and programs of organizations that otherwise may not be adequately funded to accomplish all of their goals.

The volunteer group that had been taking care of Vista House chose to formalize their standing and became a designated Friends group making them an incorporated, private, not-for-profit organization with tax-exempt status, The Friends of Vista House.

The volunteer group works in cooperation with Oregon Parks and Recreation Department (OPRD) which is responsible for all State Parks and Recreation areas, Scenic Waterways, and the Willamette River Greenway. OPRD was created as a branch of the Highway Department in 1921 and became a separate department in 1990. The state of Oregon is the owner of the Vista House and the Crown Point property, which was deeded to them by Multnomah County in 1938.

The high standards established by OPRD have resulted in the Oregon Parks system being ranked in the top ten in the nation by the country's over 40,000,000 million visitors a year.

The central focus of the Friends group is to provide interpretive and educational programs for visitors and the community, and to generate financial support to help fund their goals to care for Vista House. The primary source of funding comes from revenue earned in the Interpretative Gift Shop, espresso café, donations, and memberships. The interpretive volunteers are trained to answer visitor's questions regarding the Vista House, Columbia River Gorge, the Historic Highway, and sites of local interest including hiking trails and waterfalls. In 2012 the Friends of Vista House volunteers logged nearly 10,000 hours.

5

Destructive Forces

Although the Friends group, working with OPRD, was able to fix up Vista House enough so parts of it could be open to the public, their efforts were only temporary solutions to the deteriorating building.

The physical impact from the wear and tear of the people traffic was only part of what Friends of Vista House and OPRD were up against. The most destructive force was Mother Nature's sculpturing tool – the weather. Weather is a topic of conversation almost everywhere, but the circumstances in the Gorge are often newsworthy. The Pacific Northwest is known for its rather moderate climate, however, geology in the Columbia River Gorge often magnifies the environmental factors resulting in extreme conditions.

The most dominant feature is the wind that blows down the Gorge, very hot in the summer and very cold in the winter. Vista House, sitting on top of an exposed promontory, takes the brunt of whatever the weather gods hurl down the Columbia Gorge.

During his designing of Vista House, Edgar Lazarus took the weather conditions in to account when his plans call for,

> ...a Class A reinforced concrete structure with the superstructure to be hurricane proof and of enduring material, which would withstand the elements and wind of this exposed situation...

Had he not, Vista House would probably be sitting on the Pacific Ocean coastline. The locals tell of wind measured at 155 mph in the 1940s. On December 20, 1935 the roof and equipment of a weather station located at Crown Point (Thor's Heights) was blown away by winds estimated

Wind at Vista House—photo courtesy of Clem Bergevin

Destructive Forces

at 120 mph. It is not uncommon for winds to reach 60-70 mph with 100 mph gusts.

There are numerous stories about car doors being sprung open; glasses, scarves, and hats blown off; and people being blown down. The most sensational story was when a local news crew was at Vista House to film the effects of wind, and one reporter was blown down the stairs while the camera was rolling. The clip made national news. Winds of this nature do not happen every day, but it is not unusual to experience winds above 30 mph. Good examples of why Lancaster felt the need to build an "Isle of safety to all the visitors who wish to look on that matchless scene."

In addition to the wind, the Gorge is famous, or perhaps infamous, for its freezing rain. It is not uncommon during the

Vista House telescope in the ice—Photo courtesy of Sarah McDevitt

Vista House in the ice—photo courtesy of Sarah McDevitt

winter for the weather conditions in the Gorge to be so severe that it is necessary to close Highway I-84, the major interstate freeway running east and west along the Columbia River.

The demarcation in climate conditions between the Gorge and Portland, Oregon, is obvious when the wind and ice are so severe in the Gorge it is necessary to close the freeway, but 15 miles away in Portland it is above freezing and raining.

Other contributing factors to the decline of the building were the length of time it was vacant after its closure due to World War II, and the damage caused by vandals.

When the war broke out there was fear of West Coast coming under attack and it was thought Vista House could be a target. As a result it was closed and many of its furnishings removed and put in storage. Because it was unattended for a number of years, there was much damage from water leakage throughout the building. When it reopened, concessionaires leased the building, but were limited in their ability to adequately maintain much of the facility.

To add insult to injury, Vista House, as special as it is, had suffered at the hands of vandals: broken windows, glass bricks, and light fixtures; graffiti;

trash scattered all about; deposits of biological material; and break-ins with miscellaneous stolen items.

6

Good Intentions

Many of the attempts to fix problems actually resulted in creating more trouble. Arguably, the two most harmful attempts were covering the roof of the dome with copper to prevent leaking that instead resulted in increased seepage; and upgrading the heating system with an oil furnace that required alterations to the building that were unsightly, and produced grimy soot that settled throughout the lower level.

Although done with the best of intentions, other efforts (e.g., cementing over the glass blocks used for lighting in the basement, covering vents, and installing metal storm windows on the upper observation deck), instead of helping, only contributed to the deterioration of the building.

A letter written in 1954, by Frank Riley, who gave the address dedicating Vista House in 1918, attests to the level of disrepair at that time:

Its dome no longer lighted, the graceful and imposing monument is indistinguishable in the dark and the encircling light standards are without lamps, for one reason because as often as they are renewed they are shot at, shattered, by young vandals, the same species that befoul the roadside with trash and empty beer cans. And... the noble interior of the Vista House itself, no longer serves the purpose for which it was designed, a place in which to rest and relax and to contemplate the inspiring panorama.

Shattered window—author photo

It is now a commercial Coney Island sales room, popcorn, postcards, "novelties", cluttered clear up to the view windows; no longer a visitors' lounge, no(t) even one chair to rest in.

In 1981 after years of band-aid fixes for a multitude of malignant problems, a structural study was done as part of the Columbia River Highway Project. The study was comprehensive, evaluating both the interior and exterior of the building.

The conclusion was that, "the continual maintenance and gradual restoration of the Vista House is of the utmost importance." It was also noted that further investigation of inaccessible areas was also needed to complete the study.

Broken lamp shade—author photo

Apparently the significant word in the recommendation was *gradual* because nothing significant happened until 14 years later in 1995 when McBride Architects was selected to do a comprehensive evaluation, using current day technology, to determine the structural needs of the building. The conclusion from that study was:

> Unless treatment of problems is begun, the jewel created by Edgar Lazarus and other visionary Oregonians will continue to deteriorate until the historic materials are

destroyed and the structure itself may be compromised.

PRESENT DAY

7

Restoration

Following the McBride study it became apparent that the cost of the restoration would exceed the OPRD budget and most of the funding would have to come from private organizations and the public.

OPRD, the Friends of Vista House, and the Oregon State Parks Trust came together to combine their resources to accomplish raising $4 million dollars: $2 million for the exterior and $2 million for the interior. During the fund raising period Parks found it necessary to close Vista House to visitors in the fall of 2001 because of unsafe conditions.

As funding became available, the restoration, with oversight from the State Historic Preservation Office, began on the exterior in August 2001.

Exterior Restoration—author photo

Major damage discovered on the exterior included: deterioration of the copper roof and window frames; skylights intended for providing light in the basement covered under layers of cement; numerous problems throughout the balcony; masonry breakdown; and stone walls in disrepair. Also important to restoration was addressing the decline of the outside surface.

The problems with the exterior were major contributors to the destruction of the interior. Most of these factors contributed to the water leaks and moisture retention throughout the structure. It was not unusual for State Parks employees and volunteers to mop up to 50 or more gallons of water a day.

Some of the noticeable degradation included plaster flaking off from the ceiling and walls, pitting of the Kasota stone, and a strong odor of mold. In a

Restoration

Clockwise from top: **Interior restoration, man on scaffolding**—author photo; **Staircase work**—author photo; **Work on fountain and wall**—photo courtesy of Jim Hessel

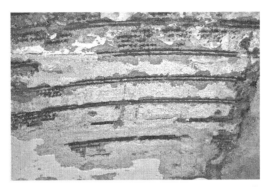

Rebar/cement damage—photo coutesy Jim Hessel

number of places the marble was cracked or had fallen off the walls and stairs. Instead of the original elegance once greeting visitors, they were assaulted with a scene of neglect and abuse. And this was only what was visible.

The 1995 evaluation also identified concealed structural deterioration, outdated electrical and mechanical systems, and a need for a new sewer system, all of which contributed to the later decision to close Vista House.

8

More Controversies

The restoration started in August of 2001 and continued until the spring of 2006. As with most construction projects, there were a number of problems, particularly with different contractors having agendas. When the first project manager, Henry Kunowski, moved to a different job, the project was handed over to Jean Castello.

It was noted a number of times that Ms. Castello functioned as much as a mediator as a construction manager. But those squabbles paled compared to those that followed during the last year of construction.

Ramp and river—author photo

One of the restoration goals was to make Vista House available to people with limited mobility. Although the federal American with Disabilities Act (ADA) has exemptions for historical structures, State Parks Administrators wanted to accommodate the intent of ADA as much as possible.

When it became publicly known that the State had decided to put a wheelchair ramp on the outside of Vista House and an elevator inside, all hell broke loose.

Feelings were mixed. Many of the volunteers for the Friends of Vista House (whose mission was to care for and protect the building) felt a ramp leading into the front door detracted from the initial impression visitors would have. And even worse would be defacing this historical national icon by cutting a hole in the marble floor and installing an unsightly elevator.

Before it was over, volunteers were sanctioned, board members resigned, and the relationship be-

More Controversies

tween OPRD and FOVH was damaged. The FOVH reactions were not about biases toward challenged individuals, but concern for the preservation of the historical nature of the building.

It was not until the major restoration work was done in April of 2004 that Parks began meetings to develop plans for a ramp and elevator that would meet ADA standards.

The reason for starting plans so late in the process was not clear to many, but having numerous agencies and commissions involved certainly contributed to the delay.

What was clear was Vista House would not be opened in 2004, as many thought it would be. The first ramp design was a failure, and other options had to be developed. Federal, State, and local agencies all had their ideas of what should happen, and the Oregon branch of the American Institute of Architects became involved.

By June 1, 2005, an acceptable ramp was almost completed, however, the drawings for the elevator (now called a lift) were still in process. This resulted in new battles, but this time OPRD and the FOVH were united in efforts to get local government to show some common sense (a concept that many thought was a quixotic undertaking.)

This time the dispute was over OPRD's request for a temporary occupancy permit. With the ramp in place people with mobility problems would be able to access the inside of Vista House for the first time in its history.

Although the lift to take people from the rotunda to the lower level was not built, the contract had been awarded.

Even so, Gresham city officials denied the request for the temporary occupancy permit, because as they stated, "the state has had more than a year to build a lift and the city is not willing to accept the risk to disabled visitors who might attempt the stairs." Consequently an angry contest erupted between city officials, the state, as well as the FOVH.

Friends of Vista House had essentially no income during the three-year closure and had secured an interest free $100,000 loan from the Meyer Trust in order to maintain their existence during the closure. Another season without income from the Gift Shop, located in the lower level, would compromise the Friend's sustainability and delay their ability to address payments for the $100,000 loan.

The FOVH and OPRD's position was that by denying all access to the now restored building there would be thousands of visitors who would not be able to experience the interior of the Vista House.

FOVH president Jim Hessel made the point in his statement "Let's not handicap everyone just because a few can't get down there…" Although part of the concern was about being able to generate income, both the Friends and Parks were also concerned about the disappointment of people who had traveled to see all of the building.

Numerous confrontational debates were reported in the local newspapers, and the bureaucratic wrangling finally ceased when an agreement was reached that would allow Vista House to open. In the end, the City of Gresham granted temporary occupancy in 30-day increments with permit fees for each increment. After four very long years Vista House was provisionally reopened on June 24, 2005.

On October 30, 2005, the building was closed for the winter, and work began on the much fought over elevator. The result is an ingenious, one-of-a-kind hydraulic lift that is essentially hidden in the floor when not in use.

The top is covered with matching marble tiles so expertly fitted that visitors looking for the lift are surprised when told they are standing on its roof, only an outline of the seam of the roof being visible.

When in use, the top of the lift rises up out of the floor to expose a mahogany and glass enclosed case. When the lift is not in use it rests on the lower level where it is screened behind a frosted glass door that makes it blend in with the rest of the building.

Lift—author photo

Gilespie Corporation, the builder of the lift, was able to accomplish the near impossible, bringing together two polarized groups. They did this by supplying a lift giving handicapped visitors access to the restrooms and all of the lower level, and doing it in such a way that those who were so adamant about not defacing the building were pleased with the result.

The best result of all is that thousands of visitors who had not been able to access the lower level in the past now benefit from all of the displays, gift and coffee shops, and, of course, the restrooms.

The reopening of the building also provided visitors with a special environment for activities such as: folk art demonstrations, weddings, musical performances by choirs and individuals, book signings, and one of the highlights, photography.

9

Rededication

Vista House is one of the most photographed icons in Oregon. On May 5, 2006, five years after its closure, Vista House was rededicated with much of the same fanfare that opened it 88 years earlier on May 5, 1918.

Numerous dignitaries and special guests were in attendance. Ted Kulongoski, Governor of Oregon; Tim Wood, Director of Oregon Parks and Recreation Department; Rick Metsger, State Senator; Patti Smith, State Representative; and representatives from the Federal Highway Administration, and Oregon Department of Transportation, to name a few.

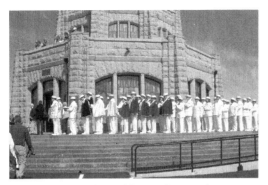

2006 re-dedication with Royal Rosarians—author photo

Portland's Royal Rosarians in their customary white suits and straw hats once again were part of the ceremonies. Antique cars from the 1918 era circled Vista House adding to the re-creation of the original dedication. Thousands of people attended, attesting to the support for saving one of America's treasures.

For nearly 100 years, Vista House has met and probably exceeded the goals of her creators by welcoming millions of visitors and providing them with a place of shelter, comfort, and inspiration.

People come to Vista House from all over the world for a multitude of reasons: to take in the magnificence of the Columbia River Gorge, to

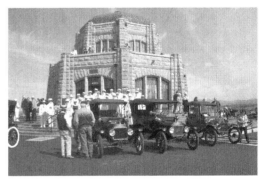

2006 re-dedication with antique cars and Royal Rosarians—author photo

learn about Vista House, the area and its history, and probably the most frequent reason of all, to utilize the restrooms.

After taking care of Mother Nature's call, travelers open their minds to the awesome environment and appreciate the elegance and craftsmanship that has gone into creating the now "multimillion dollar outhouse."

The $4.5 million dollar restoration provides all visitors with the same kind of experience as people who came in 1918. Vista House remains Lazarus' greatest achievement and Lancaster's Crown of the Historic Columbia River Highway.

APPENDICES

Appendix A

Vista House Awards

NATIONAL REGISTER OF HISTORIC PLACES

The National Register is an official list of historical sites that are recognized by the United States Government as being significant to U. S. heritage, and are important enough to qualify for public and private efforts to protect and preserve them.

The designation of a National Historic Site is derived from the Historic Sites Act of 1935 and is authorized by the National Historic Preservation Act of 1966, which is administered by the National Park Service. Receiving this designation can qualify owners tax incentives to help preserve the site. Vista House was registered in 1974.

NATIONAL TRUST FOR HISTORIC PRESERVATION'S SAVE AMERICA'S TREASURES

President Bill Clinton's Executive Order established the Save America's Treasure program in 1998. The focus of the program was to support efforts to preserve historically significant buildings, art, and published works.

The National Park Service and the National Trust for Historic Preservation administered the program. First Lady of the United Sates Hillary Rodham Clinton was the major champion of the program.

In order to be eligible for a Save America's Treasures award the properties must be considered nationally significant and possess exceptional value in illustrating or interpreting the intellectual and cultural heritage of the United States.

In 2009, First Lady Michelle Obama stated:

> Save America's Treasures invests in our nation's irreplaceable legacy of buildings, documents, collections, and artistic works. These awards empower communities all over the country to rescue and restore this priceless heritage, and ensure that future generations continue to learn from the voices, ideas, events, and people represented by these projects.

When Vista House was recognized as one of America's Treasures Dwight Young stated that, "Far from being an intrusion in the landscape, the building was designed to be -and is - an ornament to its regal perch atop the aptly named Crown Point." (Saving America's Treasures 2001, National Geographic, Washington, DC.) Vista House was designated as one of America's Treasures in 1999.

In 2011, in order to address the economic problems of the country, the U. S. Congress did not renew funding for the program.

In addition to these two specific awards, Vista House is considered as a contributing feature in numerous other designated awards: Crown Point Natural Landmark; Columbia River Gorge National Scenic Area; Federal Highway Administrations' National Scenic Byways Program; National Historic Civil Engineering Landmark; National Trails System.

Appendix B

Vista House Association Founders, 1916

H. L. Pittock, *President*
William J. Piepenbrink, *Secretary*
W. E. Conklin, *Vice-President*
Adolphe Wolfe, *Treasure*

J. C. Ainsworth
H. R. Albee
L. R. Alderman
Lee Arnett
George L. Baker
W. H. Barton
Amos F. Benson
Frank Berg
J. W. Brewer
H. C. Campbell

Paul Chamberlin
O. M. Clark
C. C. Colt
H. E. Coovert
Marshall N. Dana
D. A. Dinsmoor
J. H. Dunclove
J. C. English
Aaron Frank
George H. Himes
W. J. Hofmann
Rufus C. Holman
R. Blaine Hullock
Joseph P. Jaeger
J. H. Joyce
Samuel C. Lancaster
Julius L. Meier
F. R. Norman
C. C. Overmire
N. G. Pike
Ira L. Riggs
F. W. Robinson
C. A. Spangler
Fred Speeri
F. E. Taylor
William C. Tunks
J. E. Warlein
W. D. Whitcomb

Vista House Association Founders, 1916

William Whitfield
Mark Woodruff
William F. Woodward
John B. Yeon

Appendix C

Quotes from the Rotunda Columns and Walls

"There is a time and a place for every man to act his part in life's drama and to build according to his ideals."

Samuel Christopher Lancaster, *The Columbia: America's Great Highway* (1915)

"People who do come must not be worried or frightened at trifles; they must put up with storm and cloud as well as calm and sunshine; wade through rivers, climb steep hills, often go hungry, keep cool and good natured always, and possess courage and ingenuity equal to any emergency; they will endure to the end. A lazy person should never think of going to Oregon."

Elizabeth Wood, Oregon Trail, August 3, 1851

"I knew the wild rivers and the vacant land were about to vanish forever. And the more I considered the subject, the bigger the forever loomed."

Fredrick Remington, 1898

"The production of a work of art throws a light upon the mystery of humanity."

Ralph Waldo Emerson, "Nature", 1836

"Vista House will stand like a castle of old on the point once called "Thor's Crown."

Oregon Journal (Portland, Oregon) January 30, 1916

"I have adopted the Tudor Gothic, which, better than any other type lends itself to the calm effect of broad surfaces in connection with the massive prominence of its principal parts, analogous to the cliffs themselves."

Edgar Lazarus, architect. *Oregon Journal*, October 3, 1915

"People from all over the world come here to enjoy the pristine magnificence of the Gorge and to learn about its history and natural resources."

Friends of Vista House

"It is to be simply a great rest-house for the sight seers traveling over the wonderful road and also a place from which can be had the most beautiful view on that great scenic highway."

Addison Bennett, "Vista House" *The Sunday Oregonian*, January 30, 1916

"So prodigal has nature been with us; so lavishly has she spread her feasts at our banquet table. We have been apt to feel that these glories would be never ending."

Governor Olcott's 1921 message to the legislature.

There is an eagerness, touched at times with tenderness as one moves into the unknown. Walking the wilderness is indeed like living. The horizon drops away, bringing new sights, sounds and smells from the earth."

William O. Douglas (1898-1980)

"We live within a heritage beyond our computation. Will we tilt the cup until it runs dry or build for a day beyond our day?"

Samuel Boardman Quote from Chester H. Armstrong's History of the Oregon State Parks

"We call upon the mountains,
the Cascades and the Olympics,
the high green valleys
and meadows filled with wildflowers,
the snows that never melt,
the summits of intense silence,
and we ask that they

Teach us, and show us the Way.

We call upon the forests,
the great trees reaching
strongly to the sky

with earth in their roots
and the heaven in their branches,
the fir and the pine and the cedar,
and we ask them to

Teach us, and show us the Way."

Excerpts from a Chinook Invocation quoted in Edward Goldsmith's *The Way*

Appendix D

Pioneers Represented in Vista House Rotunda

JESSIE APPLEGATE
July 5, 1811 - April 22, 1888

Best known for his role as leader of the "Cow Column" and the wagon train that became known as the "Great Migration" of 1843. During their trip down the Columbia River both Jessie and his brother Lindsay each lost a son when their boat overturned in the treacherous waters of the river.

Later in 1846 Jessie and Lindsay joined a second party focused on finding a less hazardous southern trail. The route they took started in Fort Hall, Idaho, and followed the Humboldt River leading them to the Willamette Valley. Because of his role in establishing this route it became known as the "Applegate Trail."

Although the trail bypassed the shorter but dangerous, Columbia River route, it was never very successful after another wagon train followed Applegate's suggestions and ended in disaster, losing animals, property, and at least a dozen people.

In 1849 Applegate and his family settled in the Umpqua Valley and established what he named the Yoncalla Valley, where he became the postmaster. He was active in the Republican Party and was influential in Oregon politics, including helping shape the development of the Oregon Territory as part of the United States. He also helped elect Abraham Lincoln president.

He was elected representative of Yamhill County and served from 1845 to 1849.

ASAHEL BUSH
June 4, 1824 - December 23, 1913

At the age of fifteen Bush became an apprentice printer and supported himself in that role while he studied law. He was admitted to the Massachusetts Bar in 1850. Shortly after, Samuel Thurston, Oregon congressman, recruited Bush to move to Oregon to set up a newspaper that would counter the Republican political view espoused by *The Oregonian* and the Whig party position of the *Oregon Argus*.

Bush arrived in Oregon that same year and set up his printing press, publishing the first edition of the *Oregon Statesman* newspaper on March 28, 1851. The opposing view points, particularly between *The Oregonian* and the *Oregon Statesman*, led to a style of journalism that was contentious and often malicious and became know as the "Oregon Style" of journalism.

Bush strongly supported the idea of political parties and used his paper to influence the formation of Democratic Party of Oregon. While the other newspapers were opposed to Oregon statehood, Bush and the Democratic Party championed it, using the power of the *Oregon Statesman* to inform public opinion. He was the chairperson for the Democratic Party's central committee and a delegate to the 1892 Democratic National Convention. His position on slavery reflected that of the state's electorate, opposing slavery but excluding free blacks from the state.

Asahel Bush was the first official printer for the state of Oregon, served as a trustee of Willamette University, as regent to the University of Oregon, and as a member of the board for the Lewis and Clark Centennial Exposition,

MATTHEW DEADY
May 12, 1824 – March 24, 1893

Matthew Deady was born in Maryland and studied in West Virginia and Ohio where he passed the bar in 1847. He left Ohio for the Oregon Territory in April of 1849. He traveled the Oregon Trail, arriving in the Portland area on November 14, 1849.

He settled in Lafayette, Oregon, and began practicing law in 1850. He quickly became involved in Oregon politics and helped set up the courts and law in Yamhill County.

Deady was an early member of the Democratic Party and was elected to represent Yamhill County in the House of Representatives in 1851. By 1852 he was considered one of the leading legal minds in the territory. In 1853 he moved to and settled in the Umpqua River Valley, and helped set up the court system in four Southern Oregon counties.

He continued to advance and was elected President of the Oregon Territory Council from 1852 – 1853; the 7th Justice of the Oregon Supreme Court from 1853 – 1859; and served as the sole Judge for the

United States District Court for the District of Oregon from March 1859 until his death in 1893.

Throughout his career he influenced Oregon's legal system and wrote the state's business incorporation act. Deady authored the General Laws Of Oregon and played a critical role in codifying existing laws and making new ones.

He also assisted in establishing Multnomah County Library and the University of Oregon's law school that opened in 1884 in Portland. The school later moved to Eugene.

A testament to the influence of Judge Deady is a statement by United States Attorney General (1872-1875) and Portland, Oregon's mayor (1902-1905) George Henry Williams: "No hand has been so strongly and deeply impressed upon the legislative and judicial history of Oregon as that of Judge Deady."

JOSEPH LANE
December 14, 1801 – April 19, 1881

Joseph Lane was the first governor of the Oregon Territory, appointed in 1848 and serving until 1850. He was born in North Carolina and lived in Kentucky and Indiana before relocating to Oregon. He served in the Indiana legislature from 1822-46 when he was commissioned Colonel of the 2nd Indiana Volunteers in the Mexican War. Considered a hero, Lane was rewarded for his service when President Polk appointed him the first governor of the new Oregon Territory.

Surviving an arduous midwinter journey over the Oregon Trail, Lane arrived at Oregon City in March of 1849. One of his first official acts as governor was initiating the first census of the territory, which showed 8,785 American citizens.

He was responsible for the surrender of five Cayuse Indians accused of the murders that occurred during the Whitman Massacre. These men were found guilty and hanged. He continued to be involved with the Native American issues when he was sent to Southern Oregon to end the retaliatory violence against settlers in the area. Lane was also involved in the Rogue River Wars of 1855-1856.

Starting in 1851 Lane served eight years as Oregon's territorial delegate to Congress. In 1860 because of his pro-secessionist and pro-slavery sympathies, he was nominated for Vice President running with Presidential candidate John C. Breckinridge.

After Lincoln won the election the same aspects that helped Lane be nominated for Vice President essentially ended his political career.

Following the end of his term in the Senate in 1861 Lane retired to his home on the South Umpqua River just North of Roseburg, Oregon, where he died on April 19, 1881.

JASON LEE
June 28, 1803 – March 12, 1845

Jason Lee was born in Stanstead, Quebec, Canada and attended Wilbraham Academy in Massachusetts where he graduated in 1830. After his ordination as a Methodist minister he was assigned in 1833 to head a mission for the Flathead Indians in the West.

After arriving in Fort Vancouver in 1834 he settled on the Willamette River northwest of present day Salem, Oregon.

Lee established a school for local Indians, but was unsuccessful in both retaining students and making conversions. The school flooded at one point and the mission and the Indian Manual Training School was moved to Chemeketa in the Salem area. Following the move, a school for the white population was started and called the Oregon Institute, which later became Willamette University.

Lee sought reinforcements and returned to establish additional missions. Feeling futility from the lack of conversions to the Methodist faith his interests turned to the politics of the region. He was actively involved in the formation of a provisional government and continued his commitment to furthering educational opportunities but without the focus on Native Americans.

The lack of conversions resulted in the Methodist Church replacing Lee in 1843. While visiting at his home in Canada he became ill and died on March 2, 1845.

DR. JOHN MCLOUGHLIN
October 19, 1784 – September 3, 1857

John McLoughlin was born in Quebec, Canada, in 1784. He was a baptized Catholic but was raised Anglican. He began a medical apprenticeship in 1798, receiving his certificate on April 30, 1803. A short time later he began a medical practice that resulted in his becoming a physician for the North West Fur Company that later merged with the Hudson Bay Company (HBC.)

In 1824 he became the Chief Factor of the HBC Columbia District headquarters at Astoria, Oregon. He moved to Fort Vancouver on the Columbia River where he made friends with the Indians and was a benefactor to the settlers coming over the Oregon

Trail. After an 1828 treaty between Britain and the United States, the US/ Britain boundary was established at the 49th parallel and the HBC company moved its headquarters to Vancouver, Canada. Due to this move and other personal factors, McLoughlin retired in 1846 and moved to Oregon City, Oregon, on land to which he had made claim to while still employed by the HBC. Detractors (primarily Albert Wilson, Captain Aemithius Simpson, and Samuel R. Thurston) challenged McLoughlin's property rights and asked the Oregon Provisional Government and, later, the US Congress for protective legislation denying his claims.

Thurston, in a letter containing a number of false statements sent to the US House of Representatives, was able to influence the House to include language in sections of the Oregon Donation Land Bill that resulted in forfeiture of much of his land in Oregon City, despite having declared his intent to become a US citizen in 1849.

Following his death most of the land was returned to his heirs. In 1957 the Oregon Legislature bestowed Dr. John McLoughlin the honorary title of "Father of Oregon" in recognition of all that he contributed to formation of the state.

JAMES WILLIS NESMITH
July 23, 1820 – June 17, 1885

James W. Nesmith was born in New Brunswick, Canada, while his parents were visiting from Washington County, Maine. He lived in New Hampshire and Ohio before coming to Oregon with Marcus Whitman in 1843. After arriving in Oregon City he studied law and was admitted to the bar, soon to become the Supreme Judge of the provisional government of Oregon in 1845. After finishing his term he moved to Yamhill District and played a part in the separation of a section of the district that became Polk County.

In 1847 he was elected to the Provisional Legislature of Oregon from Polk County and continued throughout his career to influence the development of Oregon as a State. He temporarily left politics to serve, with distinction, as a captain in the Cayuse War from 1847-1848.

Returning from the war, Nesmith left for the gold fields in California, remaining for about a year. When he returned to Polk County, he purchased property on Rickreall Creek that was used to establish the first post office in Polk County, where he was postmaster from 1850-1852.

He again served in military fighting in both the Rogue River War in 1853 and the Yakima Indian War in 1855. Between these two wars he was the United States Marshal for the Oregon Territory. In 1857- 1859 he was the Superintendent of Indian affairs for both Oregon and Washington Territories.

Following Oregon's entry to the Union in 1859, Nesmith was elected United States Senator for the Democratic Party where he served from 1861- 1867. He crossed party lines when he sided with the Republicans and voted for passing of the 13th Amendment to the Constitution which abolished slavery.

Nesmith held the distinction of being the only Democrat in the Senate to vote for its passage. He then was elected to the Forty-third Congress from 1873-1875. Not seeking re-election he returned home to live out his life on his farm.

He continued to be active in community affairs and helped promote and lead the Oregon Pioneer Association.

MARCUS WHITMAN
September 4, 1802 – November 29, 1847

Marcus Whitman was born on September 4, 1802 in Federal Hollow (later to become Rushville) New York. After his mother died when he was seven, he was raised by an uncle. His teenage education was in a Congregational school.

This was the time of the Second Great Awakening when several Protestant churches proselytized through the use of revivals and where Marcus experienced a conversion. From that point forward his intention was to become a minister, but was not supported by his family.

He was unable to finance an education in the ministry so at age twenty-one he apprenticed himself to a Rushville doctor. In 1825 he enrolled in the College of Physicians and Surgeons, of the Western District of New York where he received his license to practice medicine, which he did in Canada. Later he returned to Rushville's College of Physicians to obtain his M.D. degree.

Whitman then settled in Wheeler, New York, where he became active in the Presbyterian Church and was made an elder of the Church in 1834. In 1835 he was chosen to be a missionary doctor and left that summer on reconnaissance for potential mission lands. Upon his return, he married Narcissa Prentiss who wanted to join in his mission work.

The Whitmans, along with Henry Spalding and his wife Eliza, left in 1836 with the first wagon train to travel the Oregon Trail. Having already traveled this route to scout out mission lands, Marcus was invaluable as a guide for the arduous journey.

Although Dr. John McLoughlin advised the Whitmans not to settle on the Waiilatpu site near Walla Walla, they felt it was the right place for a mission for converting the Cayuse and Umatilla Indians, and settled there anyway. Their first few years focused on bringing their culture and faith to the local Indians, but for the most part they were unsuccessful.

Also, during this time the influx of pioneers grew exponentially and the Whitman mission was known for helping people who had just traveled the Oregon Trail and were in need of assistance and supplies. With the lack of conversion of the Indians and the increase in settlers, the Whitmans changed focus toward those that they could help, the pioneers.

For the next several years Marcus and Narcissa continued to teach the natives and attend to the sick. Marcus was a good physician, but knew the native population would also use their medicine men in conjunction with his treatments.

In 1847 a measles epidemic broke out causing the deaths of half of the Cayuse population. Although Whitman tried to treat them, his success was limited due to lack of immunity to the white man's disease. In the Cayuse culture the medicine man was accountable for the life of the people he treated; if the patient died, it was O.K. for a member of the deceased's family to take the medicine man's life.

Over the years other native patients had died without repercussions, but other tensions had been mounting. The Cayuse could see the impact of the thousands of pioneers that were coming and taking their lands, all with Whitman's support of white colonization. The native people were being asked to give up their way of life in favor of one that was strange and that they did not understand.

In addition to all of these factors were the tensions between the Catholic priests and the Protestant missionaries, each vying for the souls of the native populations. Also a contributor to the tension was a half-breed, Joe Lewis, who created chaos at the mission by telling the Indians Whitman was poisoning them.

The combination of all of these influences came to a head on November 29, 1847, when members of the Cayuse nation took revenge and attacked the mission, killing Marcus and Narcissa Whitman and twelve other people. Besides the fourteen dead, fifty-four women and children (some of whom died from disease) were held captive until a ransom was paid.

A few years after the attack five men from the Cayuse tribe surrendered themselves to be tried for the deaths. The Indians' defense was their belief in the tribal law allowing the killing of a medicine man that did not save a patient because of his bad medicine. When Whitman was unable to save a number of the sick Indians the tribe believed he was practicing bad medicine and had a right to kill the white medicine man. Although the decision was controversial, they were found guilty and were publicly hanged in Oregon City, Oregon on June 3, 1850.

Although Marcus Whitman never settled in what is now the State of Oregon, he was certainly a key contributor to settling the Oregon Territory by supporting the success of the pioneers who did form the state. Ironically, his support of settlement in the Oregon Territory resulted in distrust and resentment by the native population who he had come to save.

Sources

"Access Worth Waiting for at Vista House." Editorial. *The Gresham Outlook*, 24 July 2004.

AIA Historic Resources Committee. Personal communication to Oregon Parks and Recreation Department. 3 December 2004.

Allen, John Eliot and Marjorie Burns. *Cataclysms on the Columbia*. Portland, OR, 1986.

Allen, John Eliot. *The Magnificent Gateway: A Layman's Guide to the Geology of the Columbia River Gorge*. Forest Grove, OR: Timber Press, 1979.

"Architect Demands $6868. Litigation Over Vista House Contract Counted Probable." *The Oregonian*, 25 June 1918, p. 10.

"Architect Raises Bill. Edgar Lazarus Advises State of Misreading Figures." *The Oregonian*, 20 October 1917, p. 3.

"Association Is Organized to Construct Vista House on Crown Point as Memorial to Pioneers." *The*

Oregonian, 1 January 1916. www.gesswhoto.com/or-article 1 .html 7 May 2013

Baker, Mark. "Vista House: Views of the Gorge." Albany Democrat-Herald, Corvallis (OR) *Gazette Times*, 9 July 2006, p. D5.

Bullard, Oral. *Lancaster's Road: The Historic Columbia River Highway*. Beaverton, OR: TMS Book Service, 1982.

Cochran, Dick. "Most Picturesque Comfort Station in the World." *The Valve World*. June, 1918; pp. 191-195. In-house newsletter of the Crane Co. published in the end of the 19th century and in the beginning of the 20th century.

Corning, Howard McKinley, ed. *Dictionary of Oregon History*. Portland, Oregon: Binford and Mort, 1956.

"County Pledges Aid for Vista House." *The Oregonian*, 14 November 1915, p. 10.

Cowan, Ron. "Crown Point: On a Clear Day You Can See Forever." *Statesman Journal*, 26 August 1994, p. 10-11.

Dana, Jo. "Vista House Dividend of Long-Ago Investment." *The Oregonian*, 1 May 1978. Oregon Historical Society Research Library.

Drapela, Ernie. "Official Ineptness Betrays Volunteers." *The Gresham Outlook*, 11 June 2005, p. A6.

"Erection of Vista House Held Proper." *The Oregonian*, 9 April 1919, p. 24.

"Ex-State Treasure and Lazarus Clash." *The Oregonian*, 4 April 1919, p. 6. 16 January 2011.

Fahl, Ronald. "S.C. Lancaster and the Columbia River Highway: Engineer As Conservationist." *Oregon Historical Quarterly*, Vol. LXXIV, No. 2 (June 1973), 101-144.

Frazen, Robin. ""Vista House Almost Ready." *The Oregonian*, 1 June 2005, p. 2

Friends of Vista House Interpretive Volunteer Handbook. "Vista House at Crown Point State Park Visitor Information Sheet Timeline."

Friends of Vista House Interpretive Volunteer Handbook. "Rock Work Artistry."

Friends of Vista House. 'Restoration Story." www.vistahouse.com/history/restora tion-story/, 22 September 2012

Gohs, Carl. "Mr. Lazarus Lives." *The Oregonian*, 28 December 1969, p. 123.

Gragg, Randy. "Valhalla on the Gorge." *The Oregonian*, 27 April 2003, p. D1-3.

"Gusts In Gorge Unveil" Plaque to Road Builder." *The Oregonian*, 28 October 1963, p. 17.

Harrison, John A. *A Woman Alone: Mona Bell, Sam Hill, and the Mansion on Bonneville Rock.* Portland, OR: Frank Amato, 2009.

"Highway Dedication to be Pompous Ceremony." *The Oregonian* 4 June 1916, p. 5.

Historic Columbia River Highway, Columbia River Highway Bridges. Historic American Engineering Record, HAER, OR – 56. www.columbiariverhighway.com/H ABS_HAER/columbia_river_

Historic Columbia River Highway, Crown Point Viaduct Troutdale Vicinity. Historic American Engineering Record, HAER, OR – 36C www.columbiariver highway.com

"Honor Paid Builder." *The Oregonian*, 8 June 1916, p. 16.

Irving, Doug. "Vista House Due for Big Overhaul After Summer." *The Oregonian*, 11 April 2000. Oregon Historical Society Research Library.

Irving, Doug. "Vista House Settles in for Rehab and a Long Break." *The Oregonian*, 12 October 2000. Oregon Historical Research Library.

King, Bart. *An Architectural Guidebook to Portland*. www.bartking.net 9 January 2011

Kloss, Jeanette B. "Historic Columbia River Highway Master Plan," 2006.

Kolisch, Marian. Interviews with John Yeon, December 14, 1982 – January 10, 1983. Archives of American Art's Northwest Oral History Project. http://www.aaa.si.edu/collections/ora lhistories/ oral history/yeon82.htm 29 April 2009.

Lancaster, Samuel C. *The Columbia: America's Great Highway through the Cascade Mountains to the Sea*. Atglen, PA: Schiffer, 2004.

Lancaster, Samuel C. Lancaster Photo Album 1916-1918. Oregon Historical Society Research Library.

Lazarus, Edgar. "To the Public: Facts Governing the Graft Accusation Made by State Treasure Kay Against Edgar Lazarus." Letter to the Editor, *The Oregonian*, 31 October 1917, p. 11. http://0- infoweb.newsbank.com.catalog.mult colib.org/ 30 January 2011

Lazarus, Edgar. "Mr. Lazarus Accuses Board." Letter to the Editor, *The Oregonian*, 17 December

1917, p. 6. http://0-infoweb.newsbank.com.catalog. mult colib.org. 16 January 2011.

Lynott, Robert E. "Weather and Climate of the Columbia Gorge." *Northwest Science*, Vol. 40, No. 4, 1966; 129-132. northwestscience.org/ Accessed 19 February 2013.

McArthur, Lewis A. and Lewis L. McArthur. *Oregon Geographic Names*, 7th ed. Portland, Oregon; Oregon Historical Society Press, 2003.

McBride, Richard. "Restoring a Crown Jewel." *Daily Journal of Commerce*. August 1995, pp.16-18 and 47.

Mershon, Clarence E. *The Columbia River Highway: From the Sea to the Wheat Fields of Eastern Oregon*. Self Published, Portland, OR, 2006.

Mershon, Clarence E. *East of the Sandy: The Columbia River Highway*. Self Published, Portland, OR, 2001.

Mershon, Clarence E. *Living East of the Sandy*, Vol. 2. Self Published. Portland, OR, 2003.

Multnomah County Commission Minutes, Vol. 6. 1916

Multnomah County Commission Minutes, Vol. 7, 1917

Multnomah County Commission Minutes, Vol. 8, 1917

Multnomah County Commission Minutes, Vol. 9, 1918

Multnomah County Commission Minutes, Vol. 10, 1918

The National Historic Preservation Act." http://www.achp.gov/book/sectionII .html Accessed 3 November 2004.

National Park Service. "Save America's Treasures." https://www.nps.gov/history/hps/treasures/national.htm

National Register of Historic Places Inventory-Nomination Form. Oregon State Historic Preservation Office.

Nesbit, Sharon. "Squabbling Agencies Keep Vista House Closed." *The Gresham Outlook*, 14 July 2004, pp. 1A, 2A.

Nesbit, Sharon. "Vista House Officials Stunned by Decision." *The Gresham Outlook*, 1 June 2005, p. A1

"A New Crown for Crown Point?" *Oregon Journal*, 29 June 1970, p. M 3.

Oregon Department of Transportation History Committee. "Oregon On the Move: A History of Oregon's Transportation System." http://www.oregon.gov.ODOT/CS/B SS/doc/Oregon Move_Final.pdf

Perkins, W.H. "All Portland Pays Homage to Pioneer: Vista House Dedicated at Crown Point." *The Oregonian*, 6 May 1918, p.A1 and 10.

"Plaintiffs Amazed by Their Own Suits." *The Oregonian*, 27 May 1920, p. 4.

"Plans for Highway Dedication Ready: Ceremonies to be Conducted on Crown Point." *The Oregonian*, 4 June 1916, p. 18.

Riley, Frank Branch. "Crown Point and Vista House". Dedicatory Address. 6 (sic) May 1918. Historical Society Oregon Research Library Vertical Files.

Riley, Frank Branch. Letter to Mrs. Gertrude Jensen. 15 December 1954. Oregon State Historic Preservation Office files.

Richards, Suzanne. "Faded Vista." *The Oregonian*, 10 August 1995, p. ME1

Ritter, Irene. "Vista House Friends Plan Rededication." *The Oregonian*, 28 July 1988, p. ME 1 and 10.

Senior, Jeanie. "Putting Vista House in Order." *Portland Tribune*, 14 June 2005.

Smith, Dwight A. Nomination of the Old Columbia River Highway in the Columbia Gorge to the National Register of Historic Places. Dwight A. Smith. Oregon Department of Transportation, 1984.

Spencer, Aaron. "Unknown Work By Late Portland Architect Lazarus to be Unveiled." *Daily Journal of Commerce*, 5 April 2011. http://djcoregon.com

"State Expert to Act in Road War." *The Oregonian*, 11 September 1917, p. 23

Stine, Mara "Vista House Might Open After All." *The Gresham Outlook*. 11 June 2005, p. A1

"Taxpayer's League Official Criticizes Roadmaster Yeon." *The Oregonian*, 14 October 1917, p. 6.

Teague, Edward. "Edgar M. Lazarus, Architect: Life and Legacy." http://pages.uoregon.edu/ehteague/la zarus/ 9 February 2012

Tomlinson, Stuart. "Restoring an Icon." *The Oregonian*, 10 December 2001. Oregon Historical Society Research Library.

Tomlinson, Stuart. "Vista House Supporters Seek $2 million to Finish Restoring the Columbia Gorge Icon." *The Oregonian*, 2001.

Tomlinson, Stuart. "Years Fall Away at Vista House." *The Oregonian*, 28 August 2003.

Tuhy, John E. *Sam Hill: The Prince of Castle Nowhere*. Portland, Oregon: Timber Press, 1983.

"Vista House Begun: First Earth Turned for Memorial to Pioneers." *The Oregonian*, 8 June 1916, p. 17.

"Vista House Case Ends." *The Oregonian*, 28 May 1920, p. 16.

Vista House Historic Structure Report, Columbia River Highway Project 1981 Regional Management Office. History: Nina Rapport and William Manlove.

Structure Report: Ana Beth Kovel and Patricia Fletcher. Cascade Locks, 1981

"Vista House Spirit Assures Success – Party Traverses Highway Despite Inclement Weather." The Oregonian 29 November 1915, p. 10.

"Vista House to Mark Columbia as Pioneer Memorial." *The Oregonian*, 20 January 1916, Section 5, p. 4.

"Vista House Views - 75th Anniversary Commemorative Issue." Friends of Vista House Newsletter, Summer 1992.

"Vista House Will Be Opened Today." *The Oregonian*, 5 May, 1918, p. 20.

"Work on Vista House to Start on Monday." *Portland Oregon Journal.* 9 August 1916.

Wright, David W. Response to author's letter regarding questions about the ADA work at Vista House. 25 May 2005.

Young, Dwight. *Saving America's Treasures*, National Geographic: Washington D.C., 2001.

The author combined her background in research with her love of Vista House to tell the story of one of the nation's historic icons. As a volunteer for the Friends of Vista House she has spent several years as the book selector for the Gift Shop, and has seen a need for an information book that visitors could buy to remember and share their experience at the "Crown of the Historic Columbia River Highway."

The author welcomes reader feedback and can be reached at kathleenoverton65@gmail.com.

Made in the USA
San Bernardino, CA
13 March 2016